ALONG THE WATERFRONT
FREIGHTERS AT NEW YORK IN THE 1950S AND 1960S

William H. Miller

AMBERLEY

Dedicated to those stevedores, the great dockers,
of the Port of New York & New Jersey.

Front cover: A superb Albert Brenet painting, the illustrious French artist, depicting the new *African Neptune* arriving off Weehawken, New Jersey, with the midtown Manhattan skyline in the background. (Courtesy of Moran Towing & Transportation Company)

Rear cover: Barber Lines' *Temeraire*, by Carl Evers. (Courtesy of Moran Towing & Transportation Co.)

First published 2016

Amberley Publishing
The Hill, Stroud
Gloucestershire, GL5 4EP

www.amberley-books.com

Copyright © William H. Miller, 2016

The right of William H. Miller to be identified as the Author of this work has been asserted in accordance with the Copyrights, Designs and Patents Act 1988.

ISBN 978 1 4456 5408 9 (print)
ISBN 978 1 4456 5409 6 (ebook)

British Library Cataloguing in Publication Data.
A catalogue record for this book is available from the British Library.

Typeset in 11pt on 12pt Sabon LT Std.
Typesetting by Amberley Publishing.
Printed in the UK.

ACKNOWLEDGEMENTS

The author's thanks go to the following:

Captain James McNamara and Richard Faber.

Moran Towing & Transportation Co., for supplying the front and rear cover images, and Tom Johnson for supplying the foreword.

Late Frank Braynard, late Frank Cronican, Frank Duffy, late Alex Duncan, late John Gillespie, Norman Knebel, late Vincent Messina, Richard K. Morse, Fred Rodriguez, Laurens van der Laan.

Cunard Line, Ellerman Lines, Flying Camera Inc., Hoboken Historical Museum, Moran Towing & Transportation Co., Port Authority of New York & New Jersey, Royal Netherlands Steamship Co., Steamship Historical Society of America, World Ocean & Cruise Liner Society, World Ship Society – Port of New York Branch.

FOREWORD

Just after the Second World War ended, in 1946, I joined the Meseck Towing Company. I was a deckhand on tugs. Later, in 1954, I switched over to Moran Towing Company. Tugs were my life for the next forty years.

It was a wonderful time in New York harbour. Every day brought new assignments, new ships, taking us to different parts of the great Port of New York. We sometimes handled the great liners – two or three tugs undocking the likes of the *United States*, *Queen Mary*, *Independence*, *Andrea Doria* and *Gripsholm*. I often worked on Saturdays and, in the afternoon, we'd handle the *Queen of Bermuda* and *Ocean Monarch*. We tended to handle the liners up at the West Side piers, called Luxury Liner Row. These were piers 84 to 97. But some liners berthed or sailed elsewhere – Holland America Line over in Hoboken, Incres Line down in Greenwich Village and the Grace Line in Chelsea.

But I also enjoyed handling the freighters. There were hundreds of them in those days. They'd remain in port for days at time – and at piers not only in Manhattan, but in Hoboken, Jersey City and of course over in Brooklyn. Fridays were the busiest days for freighter departures. We would handle one ship after another – and often into the night. Most steamship lines wanted the ships away – and so avoiding expensive weekend overtime.

There were the Farrell and Robin lines to Africa, Moore McCormack to South America and the Meyer and Holland America lines to Europe. Then you had American Pioneer and the NYK lines to the Far East. The list of lines is practically endless.

It all began to change, however, by the 1970s. Containerised shipping had arrived and so container ships, bigger and bigger, appeared. Mostly, they used docks over in New Jersey, at Port Newark and Elizabeth. The port itself changed. There seemed to be fewer craft – not only the conventional breakbulk freighters, but the barges and floating derricks and even the need for as many tugs.

I miss the bygone Port of New York and the ships that were part of it. Bill Miller's book on freighters of the 1950s and '60s is indeed like a great parade – a trip down memory lane. What a great cast of ships!

Tom Johnson
Carteret, New Jersey
Summer 2015

INTRODUCTION

My good friend Tony La Forgia and I had the good fortune to grow up in Hoboken, on the banks of the Hudson and just across from New York City. We are the same age and the Hudson was our stage, our magnet. We were drawn to ships and shipping activity. We watched the great liners, rode the ferries and were intrigued by freighters, those charismatic cargo ships that hinted of faraway places and unusual, sometimes exotic goods. It was our very own 'maritime theater', a great and on-going production.

Myself, I had the added advantage of my family living in the north-east corner of otherwise small, mile-square Hoboken. Just streets away were the Bethlehem Steel and adjoining Todd shipyards. In my boyhood, in the 1950s, those plants boomed, rattled, pulsated. Work, meaning repairs, and usually on cargo ships, sometimes went on around the clock. Ships came from every corner of the Port of New York for attention and care. There were American Export and American President freighters, United Fruit and Moore-McCormack, but also the likes of more distant Hellenic and Zim lines. Alone, Bethlehem Steel could handle up to fifteen ships at one time, and so the mixed gatherings of these ships was fascinating. And often, they moved about within the shipyard, going from dry dock to wet dock. Cranes hovered over the ships like surgeons at work.

Also, and directly across the Hudson, were the famed Chelsea Piers. They were crammed with freighters, mostly toward the end of the week, as cost-conscious shipping lines wanted them off and away by late Friday – therefore avoiding pricey weekend overtime for the stevedores. Grace Line, for example, which occupied Piers 57 and 58 in Chelsea, often had four sailings on Friday afternoons – one passenger liner, two combination ships and one freighter. On occasion, they'd sail within 30 minutes of one another and create a Grace Line procession as they steamed south along the river. Adjoining were the four piers used by the United States Lines and occupied by C2-Class freighters, mostly on the north-European run. They had names such as *American Reporter, American Shipper, American Traveler* and, a sort of favourite, the *American Miller*. All quite similar, these groups were only broken by the visits of one of the big Mariner Class freighters, ships like the *Pioneer Mill* and *Pioneer Ming*, which were used on the New York–Far East run for US Lines' affiliate American Pioneer Line.

Those freighters were all part of a great cast, the grand parade, glorious memories for me. They're gone now – as have many of the ship owners themselves (both Grace and US Lines are long out of shipping, as examples) – and replaced in the far different, highly grouped, hugely efficient container age. In the wake of *Along the Hudson*, the prior book published by Amberley about passenger ships in New York harbour, *Along the Waterfront* has been created as a reminder of a vast, fascinating, totally wonderful freighter fleet. It has not been my intention, however, to fill this book with facts, figures and the fates of ships, but to create something of a scrapbook of some ships and their owners. Some companies – such as the Bull Line, Standard Fruit, Torm Lines and the Booth Steamship Company – did not quite make it. But then it might be reason to create yet another book about the New York harbour of, say, fifty years ago.

But for now, the cargo has been loaded, and the lines will soon be cast. Enjoy the memory lane of *Along the Waterfront*.

Bill Miller

Secaucus, New Jersey

Maritime Day, Lower New York Bay

During the Second World War, New York harbour boomed; in 1943, there were over 900 sailings. The freight in some 430,000 boxcars was unloaded and sent into ships. There were also 500 tugs, 55 large floating cranes, 1,200 open barges, 900 closed barges, over 300 railway car floats and 75 floating crane elevators. There were countless, if sometimes unidentifiable, grey-painted troopships, transports, freighters and tankers crammed in hundreds of piers or simply waiting at anchor. Great convoys of up to 100 ships, and sometimes even as many as 150, were assembled in the Lower Bay, and all the while huge troopships like the *Queen Mary* might depart with over 15,000 soldier-passengers onboard. Even as the war ended in the summer of 1945, this great boom continued. On a single day in that same summer, the Sandy Hook pilots recorded handling 243 ships in a 24-hour period. This aerial view of the Lower Bay was taken on Maritime Day, May 1946. Many of the ships are wartime-built Liberty and Victory ships.
(Author's collection)

Chelsea Piers, New York City

Constructed in 1905–10 for the largest Atlantic liners, Manhattan's Chelsea Piers, located between West 13th and West 22nd streets, were used mostly for cargo after the Second World War. Piers 54 and 56 were leased to the likes of the Cosmopolitan Line, Belgian Line and Calmar Line, while Piers 57 and 58 were kept active with ships of the Grace Line. United States Lines was by far the greatest tenant, however – they occupied piers 59, 60, 61 and 62.

In this 1954 view, we see the brand-new $12 million Pier 57, the first New York harbour with ramps for freight as well as passenger vehicles and the only one with storage space on the roof for automobiles. The pier itself was unique – it was built on three concrete caissons (or hollow boxes), upon which the superstructure of the 900-ft-long pier rests. Two United States Lines freighters are on the left, then Grace Line's combo ship *Santa Sofia* and finally the *Santa Rosa*, a Grace passenger liner. (James McNamara Collection)

Hoboken, New Jersey

Three of the biggest piers in Hoboken, just across the Hudson from Manhattan, were rebuilt in the 1950s for the American Export Lines. Identified as Piers A, B and C, they replaced the finger piers that had belonged to the Hamburg America Line and North German Lloyd. This property adjoined two piers, at Fifth and Sixth streets, which had belonged to the Holland America Line. Beyond is the Eighth Street pier and the so-called Long Dock at Ninth Street. It was used by the likes of Denmark's East Asiatic Company. (Flying Camera Inc.)

Erie Basin, Brooklyn

Erie Basin in Brooklyn's Red Hook section was a largely enclosed basin that contained cargo piers as well as the Todd shipyard. By 2010, the piers were used as moorings for barges, tugs and other harbour craft; the shipyard has been rebuilt as a shopping mall (but, sentimentally, with four of the original cranes remaining as industrial sculptures). (Port Authority of New York & New Jersey)

23rd Street, Brooklyn

No less than six freighters of the Moore-McCormack Lines are berthed in this 1960s view of the company's brand-new terminal at 23rd Street in Brooklyn. Two Bull Line freighters are to the left as well, and half of a Hamburg America Line freighter. Behind the Bull Line ships is a freighter belonging to the Black Diamond Line, berthed at the Court Street pier. Almost all of these ships would depart in a single Friday afternoon. (James McNamara Collection)

Port Newark, New Jersey

Beginning in the 1950s, Port Newark grew steadily with its vast cargo handling areas as well as extended docking facilities. By the '60s and '70s, more and more freighter lines left the traditional, aged, often crowded and congested piers of Manhattan, Hoboken, Jersey City and Brooklyn for Port Newark and the adjoining Port Elizabeth. (James McNamara Collection)

Aconcagua II

In the early 1960s, the Chilean Line replaced aging, wartime-built freighters with a new (if final) generation of breakbulk freighters. There were three new 9,000-ton sisters that included the *Aconcagua II*. She is seen approaching on the Verrazano-Narrows Bridge, opened in November 1964, on her maiden arrival into New York harbour. (James McNamara Collection)

Admiral William M. Callaghan

Operated by MSTS, the Military Sea Transportation Service, the large freighter-transport *Admiral William M. Callaghan* is seen at the Bayonne Military Annex, a long peninsula that extended into the Lower Bay and included a military repair facility with a 1,100-ft-long graving dock. The *Callaghan* was used in far-flung military supply operations, which included voyages to northern Europe, the Mediterranean and even distant Indian Ocean outposts. The big crane in the background on the right was specially constructed in 1942 to handle large, heavy equipment on battleships. The crane was still in use over seventy years later, in 2013. (James McNamara Collection)

Adonis (right)

With a large fleet of mostly smaller cargo ships, Holland's KNSM, better known as the Royal Netherlands Steamship Company, had as many as ten sailings per month to the Caribbean and South America from their terminal at 31st Street in Brooklyn. Ships such as the 4,000-grt *Adonis*, which could carry up to twelve passengers, was used in a weekly service to Curaçao, Aruba, La Guaira, Puerto Cabello, Maracaibo and Trinidad. Another weekly run was to Port au Prince and Ciudad Trujillo. An alternate but less regular service was to Dutch Guiana and still another to Cap Haitien and Haitian out ports.

In the 1950s and '60s, Holland America Line represented the passenger business of other Dutch steamship companies through their network of branch offices in the USA and Canada," recalled Laurens van der Laan, then employed by the Holland America Line. "We had a department at Holland America in New York called Dutch World Services with a staff of seven. I handled KNSM, Royal Netherlands, with their passenger service between New York and the Dutch West Indies. These ships sailed weekly from Brooklyn. So every Thursday and Friday, I took the subway to the 31st Street pier to attend the embarkation of passengers heading for Curacao, Aruba, ports in Venezuela and Georgetown in British Guiana and Paramaribo in Dutch Guiana. The ships were very popular and usually quite full.
(Royal Netherlands Steamship Company)

17155.

African Comet (overleaf)

US-flag Farrell Lines all but dominated the south and east African freighter trade from New York in the 1950s and '60s. The primary run was to Cape Town, Port Elizabeth, East London, Durban, Lourenço Marques and Beira. A secondary service to West Africa was offered, calling at Monrovia, Abidjan, Takoradi, Accra, Lagos, Apapa, Matadi, Luanda, Lobito, Pointe Noire and Douala.

Shown arriving after her maiden voyage in September 1961, the 572-ft-long *African Comet* enters the Narrows on her way to Farrell's terminal, located at 33rd Street in Brooklyn. Afterward, she made the 6,786-mile passage from New York to Cape Town in twelve days, 16 hours and 22 minutes, at an average speed of 22.31 knots. She broke all existing records on the US–South African run. The *Comet* and her sisters also carried twelve passengers in luxuriously comfortable accommodations. (James McNamara Collection)

African Enterprise

Among the finest combination passenger-cargo liners, the eighty-two-berth *African Enterprise* and her sister *African Endeavor* offered an almost monthly service from Farrell Lines' 33rd Street terminal in Brooklyn on seven-week round-trip voyages to St Helena, Cape Town, Port Elizabeth, Durban, Lourenço Marques and turnaround at Beira. In 1957, the thirteen-night voyage from New York to Cape Town was priced at $650 in a twin-bedded stateroom. (Richard Faber Collection)

African Rainbow

Inbound from South Africa: Built in 1946 by the Federal Shipbuilding & Dry Dock Company at Kearny, New Jersey, the *African Rainbow* and her sisters were the prominent Farrell freighters in the 1950s on the South African run. They were usually berthed at the company's Brooklyn terminal, but occasionally were docked in Weehawken, New Jersey, in the shadows of the approach to the Lincoln Tunnel, to offload cargos of bauxite into railway cars. The 492-ft-long ship was retired and placed in the US Federal Reserve Fleet in 1971 as the *Rainbow*. She was scrapped two years later. (James McNamara Collection)

Agwiprincess

The corporate name Agwilines was for Atlantic, Gulf & West Indies Steamship Company. They were an American firm that carried on after the Second World War and were engaged in New York–Caribbean service. Built at Wilmington, California, in 1944 as the *Cape Spear*, this C1-Class freighter joined Agwilines in 1948 and became the *Agwiprincess*. She is seen here berthed at Pier 36, at the foot of Spring Street in Lower Manhattan, and with four barges alongside. In 1951, she joined the Ward Line and became the *Mexico*; three years later, in 1954, she was transferred to the Grace Line, becoming the *Santa Fe*. She was scrapped in 1971. (James McNamara Collection)

Ajax

Britain's Blue Funnel Line offered monthly sailings from Brooklyn's Bush Terminal to the Far East – to the Suez Canal, Jeddah, Aden, Colombo, Singapore, Port Swettenham, Penang and Djakarta. Ships used included the 7,500-grt *Ajax*. Built in 1931, the 478-footer had seven hatches and accommodations for four passengers. She berthed at Pier 33 in Brooklyn. (James McNamara Collection)

Akagi Maru

Japan resumed freighter services to New York very slowly after the Second World War. Here is NYK Line's brand-new 7,592-grt *Akagi Maru* arriving for the first time on 29 November 1951. (Cronican-Arroyo Collection)

Alaunia

The great Cunard Line, best known for its passenger liners, ran a separate cargo service to New York – from London, from Liverpool and from Glasgow. The latter was well known as the 'Whisky Run' because of its large consignments of whisky made in Scotland and brought to America. Cunard freighters also carried British-made woolens, bicycles and racehorses to New York. The *Alaunia,* which weighed in at 7,000 tons, is shown arriving in New York for the first time on 18 October 1960 and was berthed at Pier 51, at Jane Street in Manhattan. (James McNamara Collection)

Alcoa Pilgrim

Owned by the Aluminum Company of America, Alcoa Line freighters carried up to twelve passengers in West Indies and South America service from New York. The 6,500-grt *Alcoa Pilgrim* Class were assigned to the South American run, usually departing from New York for La Guaira, Puerto Cabello, Guanta, Trinidad, Georgetown, Surinam and Trinidad. Including a return to a US East Coast port, this itinerary was timed to twenty-seven days.

Back in the ship-busy 1950s at New York, the port area in Weehawken, New Jersey, was known primarily for its railways. The old New York Central Railroad controlled a good part of the waterfront from 32nd to 60th streets. There were huge freight yards, machine and repair shops, piers for tugs and others for barges (both covered and open) and even for ferries (which crossed to Manhattan's West 42nd Street until 1957) and a special dock with two sturdy cranes that handled bigger, bulkier cargos. There was even a huge grain elevator, itself something of a landmark on the western shore of the Hudson. It was finally pulled down in 1964. Occasionally, deep-sea freighters came to call. They were usually worked by steam-powered, floating derricks known locally as 'goose-neck cranes'. These cranes worked with buckets. The ships were often offloading bauxite that had come up from Trinidad and Surinam. Often, it came aboard the fine-looking freighters of the Alcoa Line or from chartered ships, often flying Scandinavian colours.

Alcoa was a fascinating company back in the fifties. In earlier times, well before the Second World War, they were known as the Aluminum Line. They were, and remained, an arm of the giant Aluminum Company of America, and thus the subsequent name Alcoa. Their ships were often painted as a product reminder with lots of silver colouring. By the 1950s they had amassed a good-sized fleet of freighters, mostly 6,800-ton C1-Class ships that had five holds and carried up to twelve passengers. They had names grouped by the letter 'P' – *Alcoa Puritan, Alcoa Pegasus* and *Alcoa Pointer*. They also had some larger, C2-Class ships, which used an 'R' nomenclature. These included the *Alcoa Ranger* and *Alcoa Roamer*. The company also had three splendid combination passenger-cargo liners, the *Alcoa Cavalier, Alcoa Clipper* and *Alcoa Corsair*, which carried up to ninety-eight passengers each. This trio sailed only out of New Orleans, however, from 1947 until 1960. They offered eighteen-day itineraries to the Caribbean.

Alcoa freighters sailed from Weehawken, Lower Manhattan, then Brooklyn and finally Port Newark (then a fledgling, pre-container marine facility in New Jersey) as well as from Philadelphia and Baltimore on sixteen- to twenty-one-day itineraries. One service went to San Juan, Mayaguez and Ponce, while the other called at San Juan, Ponce, St Thomas and St Croix. A twenty-one-night voyage was priced from $425 per person in the early 1960s.

Alcoa's chartered ships, bearing names such as *Bellavia, Maakefjell* and *Rikke Skou*, were generally used on the more extended, thirty-day round-trip service to Venezuela, Trinidad and Surinam. These were called the 'long cruises' and sailed from New York as well as Baltimore. Ports of call included the likes of La Guaira, Puerto Cabello, Maracaibo, Guanta, Paramaribo, Paranam and Moengo. Curaçao and Aruba were sometimes added as well. These full voyages were priced from $630 per person.

Alcoa also ran freighter cruises from Mobile and New Orleans, but increasingly relied on chartered, less expensive, foreign-flag tonnage. They also began offering trips on ore carriers, larger vessels that sometimes carried as few as four passengers. But like many US-flag operators, Alcoa turned fully to freight in the 1970s.

Today, the Weehawken waterfront has been totally rebuilt and gentrified with a bustling ferry service to and from Manhattan, restaurants, sports facilities and lots of luxury housing. Near the very site where Alcoa freighters once berthed, newly constructed, riverside town houses are now (2015) selling for $1 million and up.

As a notation, the 417-ft-long *Alcoa Pilgrim*, shown here arriving off Lower Manhattan, was decommissioned in 1963, mothballed for two years and then scrapped at Mobile, Alabama. (James McNamara Collection)

Alcoa Ranger (opposite)

The larger C2-Class *Alcoa Ranger* was used in the Puerto Rico and Virgin Islands trade – sailing from New York to San Juan, Mayaguez, Ponce, St Thomas, St Croix and a sugar port in Puerto Rico. This itinerary was timed to eighteen-day round trips. The *Alcoa Ranger* is shown departing Brooklyn, with Bethlehem Steel's 56th Street plant and the Brooklyn Army Terminal in the background.
(James McNamara Collection)

Alsatia (right)

The *Alsatia* is seen here docking in Red Hook, Brooklyn, in March 1952. She and her twin sister, the *Andria*, were unique – they were freighters but with two funnels. They looked like miniature liners, especially when berthed at Cunard's Piers 90 and 92, along Luxury Liner Row. Mostly, the pair was used on the London–New York freighter run.
(Gillespie-Faber Collection)

American Builder

Usually on Fridays, back in the 1950s, five or six freighters belonging to the United States Lines left the New York City docks and headed for northern Europe. There might be the *American Forwarder* going to Dublin, the *American Leader* to Glasgow, the *American Scout* for London, the *American Harvester* to Antwerp and the *American Builder* to Bremerhaven (shown here). Usually, they were cleared before midnight Friday so as to escape the high weekend overtime charges. The US Lines berths were often quite empty on weekends.

These freighters were class C-2 type design – 7,500 tons and 459 feet in length, steam turbine-driven of about 17 knots and, along with five holds of highly profitable cargos, they had space for twelve passengers, comfortably housed in six doubles, each with a bedroom and private shower and toilet. A nine-day fare to, say, Antwerp was set at $180 in 1959. The ships tended to arrive and depart from Manhattan's Chelsea Piers, numbers 59 through 62, between West 19th Street and West 22nd Street.

Vincent Love, who worked in the passenger department of the United States Lines, mostly for the luxury liners *United States* and *America*, had a stint in the late '50s of looking after the passengers aboard the freighters:

> There were five, six, even seven sailings a week and each ship was full up with twelve passengers. Lots of travellers liked them. They were less fancy than the liners and offered a more casual, relaxed way to and from Europe. Once, one of the freighters broke down outside New York and had to return to the Manhattan piers. I bought copies of the *Journal American* and that pleased them. They read while the repairs were made.

In the 1950s, Miles MacMahon served as a radio officer aboard three of these ships: the *American Scout, American Forester* and *American Producer*. 'They were classic American freighters of that time,' he recalled.

But they were also modified sometimes to suit their trades. The *American Scout* was specially fitted to go up the Manchester Ship Canal in England. The stacks and the masts were on hinges and so could be lowered for bridge clearances. United States Lines' ships were kept in tip-top condition, always immaculate. They used the Chelsea Piers, Nos 59 through 62, on Manhattan's West Side. Inbound from Europe, the ship would discharge cargo first at New York and then go off on a seven- to ten-day 'coastal swing' – calling at Boston, Philadelphia, Baltimore, Norfolk and Charleston. Then they would return to New York to finish loading for a return to Europe. All cargo was loaded in pallets and nets. There were no containers then.

Miles MacMahon was somewhat unique – he worked part-time, in the summers only, as a ship's radio officer. He was a high school physics teacher in New Jersey for the other 9 months. 'I made $5,000 a year teaching in 1960,' he recalled, 'but made more than that for three summer voyages on United States Lines. We'd sail to various ports – Hamburg, Bremerhaven, the King George V Docks at London. We also have other, special sailings. On the *American Producer*, I recall once going to western Europe – to St Nazaire in France and to Bilbao and Santander in Spain. There were three-week round trips. We carried twelve passengers on each ship and, in summer, we had lots of teachers onboard.'

When US Lines began adding newer, larger freighters in the early '60s, passenger quarters were not included. This disappeared after the older ships were retired, many of them finishing up on supply runs to Southeast Asia during the Vietnam War and then, aged and exhausted, finished their days at Taiwanese scrapyards. (James McNamara Collection)

American Challenger

The 1960s was an era of rebuilding, renewal and improvement for many freighter companies. The sleek, 21-knot cargo liner *American Challenger* arrived for a tug and fireboat reception on 28 August 1962. The 11,105-grt vessel, with a resemblance to the superliner *United States*, the fastest passenger ship afloat, sailed within three days on her maiden crossing to Le Havre and London. She was the beginning of a new, super-express service for United States Lines that cut two days off the passage of the average freighter. The *Challenger*'s record run was between the Ambrose Lightship and Bishop Rock in England in 4 days and 23 hours. On her very first eastbound crossing, she averaged 24.42 knots. (James McNamara Collection)

Andrew Jackson

'Waterman Steamship Company was based in Mobile, Alabama,' according to Captain James McNamara, 'but ran services from New York – including New York to Puerto Rico. Their services actually spanned the world and included military ocean cargo. Consequently, Waterman freighters – such as the *Andrew Jackson* – were often seen berthed at the Brooklyn Army Terminal or the Bayonne Military Ocean Terminal. Waterman actually remain in business [2015] and is part of International Ship Holding, which owns over fifty ships.' (World Ship Society)

Andyk

Photographed in June 1949, the American-built *Andyk* was part of post-war aid and reconstruction to Holland, namely to the Holland America Line. 'Westbound to the States, we carried tulips, caraway seeds, agricultural products, cheeses and lots of Heineken beer,' remembered the late Captain Cornelius van Herk, who served aboard about a dozen Holland America freighters in the late 1940s and '50s. 'Going back to Holland, we carried American-manufactured goods, machinery, tin plate and lots of grain that was loaded by floating elevators. We later expanded this service, in August 1949, to Germany, to Bremen and Hamburg. These were our first German calls since before the War.'

'While their liners were known as the Spotless Fleet so too were Holland America's cargo ships, including Victory Class freighters,' added Captain James McNamara. 'Their ships always had that clean, soapy smell. They were always well maintained. I remember Holland America also carried lots of heavy-lift cargos.' (Cronican-Arroyo Collection)

Angela Fassio

'Fassio Line ships docked over in Brooklyn and later in Port Newark [shown here],' remembered Captain McNamara. 'Their ships each had a family name, like the *Angela Fassio*, and sailed in Mediterranean–New York service. They carried lots of Italian products on their westbound voyages. Fassio disappeared, however, in the face of greater containerisation in the 1970s.' (Moran Towing & Transportation Company)

Antarctic Ocean

Departing from Jersey City's Harborside Terminal, the *Antarctic Ocean* – sailing for the Swedish-Orient Line for Australian and New Zealand ports – had a rather unique combination of derricks/booms and cranes. 'Scandinavian ships often had wooden bridges,' noted Captain McNamara. 'The wood reduced distracting the ship's compasses as well as being lighter than steel and therefore easing the weight of the ship.' (James McNamara Collection)

Asia

Cunard often used its liner piers, 90 and 92, at West 50th and 52nd streets, for their freighter services. A freighter might be berthed amid the likes of the *Queen Mary* or *Queen Elizabeth*, *Mauretania* and *Caronia*. Here the 8,700-grt *Asia* arrives on her maiden call in 1947. She will be docked at Pier 90.

'Ships such as the *Asia* had long, low superstructures and almost hinted of a larger passenger capacity, say for fifty to a hundred passengers,' added Captain McNamara. 'Instead, there was a cargo hold amidst the superstructure, placed just forward of the funnel.' (James McNamara Collection)

Astoria Maru

For photo purposes, usually during a maiden arrival, ships were often positioned off Governor's Island in the Upper Bay, in full view of the Lower Manhattan skyline. The *Astoria Maru* belonged to Japan's Mitsubishi Lines. 'Mitsubishi had three 'diamonds' on their funnels,' added Captain McNamara. 'They have long since been merged into huge container operations and their holdings include shipyards, insurance and much else.'
(James McNamara Collection)

Attleboro Victory

Just after the Second World War, many Liberty, Victory and other standardised freighters did stints of commercial service and wearing the colours of well-known shipping lines. Here, the 1945-built *Attleboro Victory* is wearing the funnel colours of United States Lines. She is inbound at the Chelsea Piers, arriving from north European ports. The 455-ft-long *Attleboro Victory* later joined the Prudential Lines, but then served on the New York–Mediterranean run. (World Ship Society)

Arizona

The Swedish Transatlantic Line, officially known as Transatlantic Rederi, offered weekly service between New York, Gothenburg, and added Baltic ports with a stop at Boston en route. Their classic-looking *Arizona* dated from 1961 and had a rather unique design for the time: four cargo holds forward of the deckhouse and a fifth in the stern.
(Gillespie-Faber Collection)

Barber Terrier

Using Norwegian-flag freighters usually from the Wilhelmsen Lines, a US passenger and freighter operation was known as the Barber Lines. A busy and very profitable run, there were up to three sailings a month from Brooklyn via Newport News and Charleston to the Canal Zone, Los Angeles, San Francisco, Manila, Hong Kong, Yokohama, Kobe, Singapore, Bangkok, Saigon, Djakarta and finally Singapore. The rebuilt, lengthened *Barber Terrier* is seen in the foreground, on the left. In the background, in mid-stream, is the New York State Maritime Academy's training ship *Empire State*.

The old finger piers of Brooklyn Heights were replaced in the 1950s and early '60s by more modern, efficient terminals built by the Port Authority of New York & New Jersey. These 700-ft-long piers were in use until the 1980s and were later partly demolished to be made over as parkland and recreational space. (Port Authority of New York & New Jersey)

Black Swan

Using Norwegian-flag freighters that carried considerable cargo and up to twelve passengers, the Black Diamond Line was part of the virtual armada of cargo vessels that regularly departed from New York on Fridays so as to avoid expensive weekend overtime on the docks. Using ships such as the 17-knot *Black Swan*, Black Diamond serviced northern Europe – crossing to Antwerp, Rotterdam, Amsterdam, Hamburg and Bremen. (Gillespie-Faber Collection)

Campero

In its services to the east coast of South America, terminating at Buenos Aires, the Argentine State Line was often assisted by the ships of another national shipowner, the Dodero Line. Here we see the 7,600-ton *Campero*, a former Victory ship. (Gillespie-Faber Collection)

City of Auckland

One of New York's biggest and busiest shipping agencies, Norton Lilly & Company, represented a consortium of British shipowners that ran a service to Australia and New Zealand. These included the Federal Line, Port Line, New Zealand Shipping Company and the Ellerman Lines, which had a vast fleet of 'City ships' such as the 8,200-ton *City of Auckland*. She is shown here at Port Newark, in a photo dated 15 December 1970. (Gillespie-Faber Collection)

City of Brooklyn

The Bush Terminal in Brooklyn had eight long piers, eighteen warehouses and its own railway system. Built in 1905, it continued in operation until the 1970s. Among the tenants was the Ellerman Lines. Here we see the brand new *City of Brooklyn* arriving at the Bush Terminal in Brooklyn for the first time. Dalzell tugs assist the new vessel in this June 1949 view. (Ellerman Lines)

City of Chester

Inbound from distant ports in Australia and New Zealand, the 8,380-ton *City of Chester* has passed under the Bayonne Bridge, assisted by two Dalzell Towing Company tugs and bound for Port Newark.
(James McNamara Collection)

Ciudad de Barranquilla

Shown here on her maiden call in 1958, the *Ciudad de Barranquilla* was one of many sisters operated by Grancolombiana, a consortium company from Colombia, Ecuador and Venezuela. Their ships berthed along the East River, first in Lower Manhattan and then over in Brooklyn Heights. They offered weekly sailings to Colombia, Ecuador and Peru. Captain McNamara noted, 'They were actually owned by a huge coffee group and so their main northbound cargo was coffee.'
(James McNamara Collection)

Ciudad de Santa Marta

Also photographed on her maiden arrival in New York in 1977, the 11,693-grt *Ciudad de Santa Marta* and her sisters were the last new ships built for Grancolombiana. In the 1980s, the company was dissolved as the coffee groups were disbanded and coffee itself began being shipped in containers.
(James McNamara Collection)

Chungking Victory

Seen off Lower Manhattan and the World Trade Center, the Victory freighter *Chungking Victory* belonged to the China Union Lines. She was used in US East Coast–Far East service. (Gillespie-Faber Collection)

Colombia

Denmark's Det Forenede was known in US East Coast shipping circles as the United Steamship Company Limited. Among the services were four monthly sailings between New York and Copenhagen. But something went wrong with an arrival of the 5,100-grt *Colombia*. On a June afternoon in 1950, she was rammed off Brooklyn's Bay Ridge Flats by American Export's outbound *Excalibur*. The *Colombia* caught fire and began to flood; the combo liner *Excalibur* took on water and was down at the bow. Both ships had to be assisted by tugs, fireboats and barges, and were later moved to shipyards. (Frank O. Braynard Collection)

Covadonga

The Spanish Line, or more formally Compañía Transatlántica Española, offered monthly sailings in the 1950s and '60s on the twin 10,200-grt passenger combo liners *Covadonga* and *Guadalupe*. Each ship carried to 353 passengers, divided as 105 in First Class and 248 in Tourist. In the mid-1950s, they were routed between Bilbao, Santander, Gijón, Vigo, Cádiz and New York, and then onward to Havana and Vera Cruz before reversing the itinerary. The *Covadonga* is seen here arriving in the Upper Bay on a morning in March 1959. (Gillespie-Faber Collection)

Don Antonio

On her maiden voyage to Port Newark, the 8,500-grt *Don Antonio* served with the United Philippine Lines. The company offered a monthly service between New York, other East Coast ports and then through the Panama Canal to Manila, Hong Kong and Yokohama. 'United Philippine never quite made it into containers and so disappeared,' added Captain McNamara. 'Their ships would bring pineapples and lots of palm oil carried in tanks into New York.' (Port Authority of New York & New Jersey)

Drammensfjord

Seen maiden arriving on her maiden voyage in New York on 4 May 1955, the *Drammensfjord* became a regular on the run between Norway and New York. 'She was a very solid, well built, ice-strengthened ship,' recalled Captain McNamara. 'She had a classically Norwegian-style wooden bridge front and with her crew quarters placed aft in a "three island" set-up. She also has very nice accommodations for a dozen passengers.' (James McNamara Collection)

Empire Star

Although best known for their UK–South America operations, Britain's Blue Star Line was part of a consortium that ran a New York–Australia and New Zealand service. Carrying general cargo outbound and refrigerated goods (mostly chilled meats) on the return voyages, big freighters such as the 11,085-ton *Empire Star* were used in this service. She is seen here loading at the Brooklyn Port Authority piers. (James McNamara Collection)

Equateur

Like Cunard, the French Line was best remembered for its luxurious Atlantic liners. In the 1950s, this was headed by the famed *Île de France* and *Liberté*. The Paris-headquartered company also operated freighters, such as the 1951-built *Equateur*, shown berthed at the Port Authority Grain Elevator at Columbia Street in Brooklyn. She sailed in regular service to Le Havre and Bordeaux. (James McNamara Collection)

Esparta (opposite, top)

In the mid-1950s, business for the United Fruit Company, sometimes referred to as Fruitco, was booming. The company had fifty-five ships that carried 41,000,000 stems of bananas each year, many of these into New York harbour. Ships such as the 7,200-ton *Esparta* would arrive from Caribbean and Central American ports and then tie-up at United Fruit's specially built (in 1950) 'banana exchange' terminal. The bananas would be offloaded by special conveyor cranes and transferred to refrigerated railway freight cars and freezer-cooled trucks. Once fully unloaded, the 459-ft long *Esparta* would then be 'shifted' to the company's Lower Manhattan piers for reloading but with general cargo. United Fruit had three to four departures each week.

At the age of twenty-five and with rising operational costs, many American freighters were either retired or sold to foreign owners. The *Esparta*, which was first commissioned in September 1945, was transferred to a United Fruit affiliate, Elders & Fyffes Ltd, and placed under the British flag in 1970. She was renamed *Toloa*, sailed for another seven years and then was sold to scrappers on Taiwan. Her career spanned thirty-three years. (Gillespie-Faber Collection)

Eurybates (opposite, bottom)

Loading at Pier 1, located at the foot of Fulton Street in Brooklyn Heights: the 6,800-ton *Eurybates*, owned by the Greek-flag Marchessini Lines, sailed between New York and Mediterranean ports. (Gillespie-Faber Collection)

Exemplar

I especially remember them from their comings and goings and, of course, from being at dock in my hometown, at the bottom end of the waterfront of Hoboken, New Jersey. It was just across the mighty Hudson River from the famed Manhattan skyline. The American Export Lines had three piers, quite a distinction in the very busy, ship-filled and often crowded New York harbour of the 1950s. They were leased from the Port Authority of New York & New Jersey. Pier A, at the foot of First Street, was for inward cargo; Pier B in the middle was for both inward as well as outward; while Pier C at Fourth Street was only for outward goods. Piers A and C had been newly built (in the mid-1950s) and could handle three freighters at one time, while Pier B, the longest at about 1,000 feet from end to end, had been refitted and upgraded after a long, colourful history. Built back in 1905, it had welcomed some of the great pre-First World War ocean liners that belonged to the Hamburg America Line and the North German Lloyd. Some of the largest, most luxurious ocean liners afloat once berthed there.

Business for American Export was booming in the '50s. In all, there were about two dozen freighters in the company fleet, many of them standardised ships, belonging to the 8,500-ton, 459-foot-long Exporter Class. They each had names beginning with 'Ex' – such as *Express, Expeditor, Exemplar* (shown here), *Exminster* and *Excellency*. Along with lots of freight, many of them carried up to twelve passengers as well. There were other, different ships as well – like *Exton* and *Exmouth*, which were Victory Ships from the Second World War. A few of these carried up to six passengers, but all in the same cabin and tickets were sold only to male passengers. Export also ran two large, luxurious liners, the 1,000-passenger sister ships

Independence and *Constitution,* both of which were completed in 1951. The company also had the so-called 'Four Aces', a quartet of passenger-cargo ships that carried 125 all-First Class travellers and which were named *Excalibur, Excambion, Exeter* and *Exochorda.*

With a fleet of some thirty different ships, all used on the Mediterranean and Middle East runs, it was said that an American Export vessel passed through the Straits of Gibraltar every 24 hours. 'The Mediterranean was our primary run, the backbone of the Company,' remembered Robert Capello, who worked in both the company's freight and passenger departments, both located in their Lower Manhattan offices,

> Our long-haul freight service was through the Suez Canal to India, Pakistan, Ceylon and Burma. I remember that, in the 1950s and '60s, we carried lots of rags out to Bombay, but returned with finished clothing. There were also lots of spices and teas going to the States. From the Mediterranean, we brought cans of olive oil and leather goods from Italy, wines from Spain and oranges from Israel. Over to Europe, we transported lots of American manufactured goods: machinery, automobiles, trucks, locomotives and even household appliances like stoves and refrigerators.

American Export freighters regularly sailed to the likes of Lisbon, Cádiz, Barcelona, Marseilles, Genoa, Tunis, Piraeus, Salonika, Iskenderun, Haifa, Alexandria, Bombay and Karachi. Typically for freighters of that era, they did the so-called 'East Coast swing', as it was called. While the longest stays were at New York (Hoboken), they also called for additional cargo at Boston, Philadelphia, Baltimore and Norfolk/Hampton Roads.

In 1960, American Export bought out another US-flag shipping line, the Isbrandtsen Company, and together they had over forty ships. Noted especially for its eastbound around-the-world service with freighters with 'Flying' names, such as *Flying Gull* and *Flying Enterprise*, the two firms were soon renamed, by 1962, as the American Export-Isbrandtsen Lines.

By the mid-'60s, there were great changes in shipping as the containerisation began. It was now all more efficient and required different, more purposeful vessels. Export was a forerunner and began by converting two bulk carriers to carry up to 660 20-foot cargo containers. Soon, Container Transport Lines was a specially created subsidiary and early experimentation even included the loading of containers by helicopter!

The company also dabbled in nuclear power by chartering (from the US government) the world's first nuclear merchant ship, the 14,000-ton, sixty-passenger *Savannah*. They leased this $60 million ship, intended to be a prototype of many, for $1 a year from the Federal Maritime Administration. Export even proposed a fleet of as many as thirty 'nuclear super ships' to strengthen and also revive the already sagging American merchant marine. Sadly, however, the 595-ft-long *Savannah* proved to be very expensive as well as difficult to operate. Also, because of the potential risks with her reactor, she was not always welcome in foreign ports. Many harbour officials even insisted, for example, that the ship dock stern-in so as to make a quick, emergency getaway if needed. She sailed only for six years before being made over as a museum ship. Presently (in 2015), after being 'mothballed' for some years near Norfolk, she is waiting in Baltimore, supposedly to be restored as a floating museum, but moored near Washington, DC.

American Export also built new break bulk freighters and then purposeful containerships in the 1960s, but gradually faced declining markets. Less expensive, foreign-flag tonnage was now a big problem, for example. Downsizing, the company left Hoboken in 1970 and relocated to smaller New York harbour terminal operations at the Bush Terminal in Brooklyn. In 1978, the company was bought out by another American shipowner, the Farrell Lines, and soon lost its identity. In 2000, Farrell itself was bought out by P&O-Nedlloyd, the British-Dutch shipping giant (itself now owned by Denmark's Maersk Line), and was reduced to but a few ships as the Farrell Mediterranean Express. One of the last former Export ships, the *Argonaut,* was used on the ammunition run out to Iraq. Another, the *Export Banner*, went to scrap in Texas in 2007. The long gone, but still wonderful ships of American Export are these days left to the history books.

The 473-ft-long *Exemplar* is seen here at Pier A being loaded by a unique craft: a floating grain elevator. (James McNamara Collection)

Exermont

At anchor in the Lower Bay, the *Exermont* was typical of the C3-Class of freighters owned by American Export. 'She had a large layout including deep tanks,' noted Captain McNamara. 'These tanks were often used to carry the likes of Spanish olive oil. Export's Hoboken piers were often crammed with barrels of olive oil.' Appearing to be larger, the *Exermont* weighed in at 6,400 gross tons. (James McNamara Collection)

Export Agent

Built in 1961, *Export Agent* and her three sisters – *Export Ambassador*, *Export Aide* and *Export Adventurer* – were 'lovely, very handsome ships' according to Captain McNamara. They were like modern versions of the 'Four Aces', which carried 125 passengers. The *Agent* and her sisters, the beginning of a massive $436 million rebuilding program, had space for twelve passengers. Seen here outbound in the Lower Bay, the *Export Agent* was later transferred to the US military and converted to an ammunition ship.
(James McNamara Collection)

Export Ambassador & Export Aide

The 493-ft-long *Export Ambassador* is berthed bow out at Pier B in Hoboken while her twin sister, the *Export Aide*, is being docked at Pier C. (Moran Towing & Transportation Company)

Export Banner

Shown at Pier B in Hoboken, the *Export Banner* was one of a new class of freighter built by American Export in the early 1960s. They had a gross tonnage of 7,900 and measured 493 feet in length. 'They were very functional ships, built just prior to containerisation and so not suited for the container age. They were among the first, modern generation, engines-aft cargo vessels and were suited to carrying heavy cargos such as bulldozers and locomotives. They were redundant far too soon, however. Only in later years, they could carry some containers on deck.' (James McNamara Collection)

Fernfield

Headquartered in Lower Manhattan but using mainly Norwegian-flag freighters such as the 1948-built *Fernfield* (owned by Norway's Fearnley & Eger), the Barber Steamship Lines had up to six separate operations. One of them was Barber-Fern-Ville Lines, which offered twice-monthly sailings westward around the world – returning from Colombo and Port Said to New York.

In this nighttime view, there's trouble: one of the hatches aboard the *Fernfield*, docked in Brooklyn, has caught fire. (Cronican-Arroyo Collection)

Fernriver

Another arm of Barber Steamship Lines' vast operation was Fern-Ville Mediterranean Lines. Using ships such as the 2,800-grt *Fernriver*, the base itinerary was New York to Casablanca, Genoa, Naples, Alexandria, Beirut, Piraeus and Istanbul.
(James McNamara Collection)

Flying Enterprise

Isbrandtsen Line ran a sizeable fleet of freighters, all carrying breakbulk cargo and four to twelve passengers on three- and four-month around-the-world voyages. Their Victory Class ships had two four-bunk rooms and these were offered only to male travellers. After leaving their Brooklyn berths, they sailed to the Caribbean, passed through the Panama Canal and then crossed to the Far East and Southeast Asia. Finally, they returned home via the Suez and the Mediterranean. The *Flying Enterprise* made worldwide headlines when she foundered, in January 1952, after a long, heroic rescue effort during which her master remained onboard until the final moments. (Gillespie-Faber Collection)

Flying Spray

The *Flying Spray* is in the foreground, berthed on the north side of Pier C in Hoboken during an ailment common to US-flag shipping: strikes. No less than eight American Export-Isbrandtsen ships are idle during a costly, schedule-disrupting strike in the winter of 1963. (James McNamara Collection)

Geneve (below)

Whistles sounded and fireboats sprayed! It was the maiden arrival of a rather unusual vessel in May 1960: the Swiss-flag *Genève*. Operated by the CTO Line and represented by the Black Diamond Lines, the 9,200-ton ship was owned by Keller Shipping Limited of Basel. She was given a welcome that included a sailing along the Hudson to Pier 88 and then assignment to Pier 1, at the foot of Court Street in Brooklyn. (James McNamara Collection)

Goran Kovacic (opposite)

'Jugolinija had mostly secondhand ships in the 1950s, but then began new tonnage,' recalled Captain James McNamara. 'Their new ships were quite lovely and very modern for their time [such as the *Goran Kovacic*]. Jugolinija lasted into the container age, but then was dispersed following the break-up of Yugoslavia.' Typically, the 7,500-grt *Goran Kovacic* is seen off lower Manhattan during her maiden arrival in 1967. (James McNamara Collection)

Gorredyk (opposite)

Containerised shipping was on the horizon, even if the distant horizon. The 7,200-ton *Gorredyk* was one of four sisters, the 'G Class', built by Holland America Line between 1960 and 1963. These 534-ft-long ships were the company's last conventional, breakbulk freighters. Seen here berthed at Pier 40, which opened in March 1963, French artist Albert Brenet is painting the *Gorredyk* for a cover for *Towline*, the house magazine for Moran Towing & Transportation Company. Looking on, Holland America executives are to the right.
(James McNamara Collection)

Gopher State (below)

The US's Marine Lines named their ships after the nicknames of American states. Running services to northern Europe, the Mediterranean and around the world, ships such as the C3-Class, 492-ft-long *Gopher State* (seen here in April 1972) were familiar sights in New York harbour. Sometimes there were problems, however. On 21 October 1950, the *Pelican State* rammed the East Asiatic Company's passenger-cargo liner *Erria* off Ambrose Light. A Victory ship, the *Pelican State* had a damaged bow.
(James McNamara Collection)

Great Republic

The 11,757-ton *Great Republic*, seen off the Brooklyn shoreline, had four sisters – the others being *Red Jacket, Resolute* and *Young America* – and was built in the late 1960s. 'They were, unfortunately, among the biggest misfits,' according to Captain McNamara. 'They began as general cargo ships with ro-ro ramps over the stern for Moore-McCormack Lines' New York-Northern Europe service. The ships had to dock stern-first and directly to the pier head because of this ramp. Consequently, these ships had lots of union problems and so were later moved over to American Export Lines and then to the newly formed Mediterranean Marine Lines. They were still never efficient enough, however. As ships, they tried to be a little bit of everything. They were actually more successful in their after lives, as military ships. In fact, two of them are still sailing [2015] – as the *USNS Curtiss* and *USNS Wright* – as aircraft logistic vessels.' (James McNamara Collection)

Hannover

The Hamburg America Line, revived after their devastation in the Second World War, offered weekly sailings in a joint service with the North German Lloyd between New York, Bremen and Hamburg. Usually, there were also calls at Antwerp and Bremen. Maintained by six twelve-passenger freighters, there were two special sailings in the spring of 1955 when the eighty-six-passenger combo liner *Hannover* crossed to New York. She is seen here off Lower Manhattan just before docking at Hamburg America's Pier 1, at the Continental Piers in Brooklyn. A luxury ship with fine appointments and facilities, the 530-footer was built for the Europe–Far East service.

The $4,000,000 ship made news on her first arrival – she was the first newly built German passenger ship to put into New York since 1939. She arrived with forty-eight passengers and a 10-ft giraffe, which was en route to the Seattle Zoo. During that maiden crossing she encountered severe weather, however, including fog, thunder storms, hail and snow, and was forced at one point to reduce speed to a scant 3 knots. She actually arrived in New York 24 hours late. Later in her career, she traded regularly to New York as the *Oriental Warrior* for the Orient Overseas Line.
(James McNamara Collection)

Har Ramon (above)

Seen on her maiden arrival in October 1961, the 6,400-ton *Har Ramon* belonged to El Yam Limited of Haifa. Using Pier 13 on the East River, she was operated by New York-based Maritime Overseas Corporation and used to carry bananas northbound from Ecuador and then general goods on her southward trips. Built at Hamburg, she was part of post-war West German reparations to Israel. (Gillespie-Faber Collection)

Hawaiian Banker (opposite)

The Isthmian Lines ran a joint service with another American shipowner, the Matson Line, from New York to Hawaii via the Panama Canal. The 492-ft-long *Hawaiian Banker* is being docked at Isthmian's terminal on the long, outer arm of Brooklyn's Erie Basin. Five US Navy ships are in the background, docked at the Todd Shipyard and being readied for service in the war out in Vietnam, in this mid-1960s view. (James McNamara Collection).

Havskar

Oslo-based P. Meyer traded as the Meyer Line and used berths in Brooklyn Heights. Noted for their smart-looking freighters each having a *Hav* name, the company had, until the 1960s, almost weekly sailings to Antwerp, Rotterdam, Bremen and Hamburg. The ten-day crossings to Antwerp were available to six-twelve passengers for $200 per person in the late 1960s. Meyer was based at the Brooklyn Port Authority piers. Here we see the *Havskar* with the *Ciudad de Barranquilla* of Grancolombiana on the left. (Gillespie-Faber Collection).

Heina

Norwegian shipowner A/S J. Ludwig Mowinckels Rederi traded to New York as the Cosmopolitan Line. Their smart-looking ships – with names such as *Horda*, *Ronda*, *Lista* and *Heina* (shown here) – offered weekly sailings, mostly on Fridays, from Manhattan's Pier 56. They were routed to Le Havre, Antwerp and Rotterdam. Cosmopolitan was among those companies that faded in the ongoing era in the mid-1960s of containerisation, however.
(James McNamara Collection)

Hellenic Pioneer

The Greek-flag Hellenic Lines maintained a large fleet, which included wartime-built Liberty ships, for its two primary services – to the Mediterranean and to the Middle East and India. Hellenic's terminal was at the lower end of the Brooklyn waterfront, at the foot of 56th Street, and often included four or five company ships at berth at the same time. The *Hellenic Pioneer* is seen arriving off 56th Street in Brooklyn in 1962.
(James McNamara Collection)

Hellenic Pride

'Built in Japan, the *Hellenic Pride* was the first of a series of sisters for Hellenic Lines' US East and Gulf Coast–Middle East service,' noted Captain McNamara.

They carried lots of jute and burlap as their main cargo on homeward voyages from India. But similar to other Greek families in the shipping business when Pericles Callimanopulos, owner of Hellenic Lines, died in the early 1980s, his sons fought over the company. Furthermore, after the fall of the Shah of Iran in 1979, US trade to Iran collapsed. Then big, US oil companies pulled out and the shipping trade, especially of oil-related machinery, all but vanished. This spelled the end for Hellenic Lines as well as others like the German-flag Hansa Line.
(James McNamara Collection)

Henry St G. Tucker

Seen berthed in Brooklyn Heights, the Liberty ship *Henry St G. Tucker* is seen in the late 1940s, doing military cargo service to ravaged, postwar Europe. (Norman Knebel Collection)

Heredia

In dry dock at Bethlehem Steel in Hoboken, this trim United Fruit vessel was having a 'haircut and shave', the expression for a quick hull cleaning, painting and light repairs. (Port Authority of New York & New Jersey)

Hibueras

Almost yacht-like with her smart appearance – an all-white hull, counter stern and raked masts and funnel – the *Hibueras* was one of nine fully refrigerated sister ships built for United Fruit Company in 1946/7. These 5,000-ton ships were constructed by Bethlehem Steel Corporation at their Sparrow's Point, Maryland, plant and could carry over 100,000 bunches of bananas in their refrigerated and insulated spaces. They were designed to service Caribbean and Central American ports, carrying general cargo outbound and returning mostly with bananas. Popular with retirees and teachers on summer holidays, these ships had comfortable quarters for up to twelve passengers. (Gillespie-Faber Collection)

Hibiscus

After the famed Furness-Bermuda Line pulled out of weekly New York–Bermuda service in November 1966, the Bermuda Express Service was formed but for cargo only. Using three small ships – the *Hibiscus*, *Poinciana* and *Oleander* – these ships made weekly departures. The 1,900-grt *Hibiscus* is seen here loading cargo at Pier 34, at the foot of Spring Street in Lower Manhattan. (James McNamara Collection)

Hoegh Dyke

Norway's Leif Hoegh operated as the Hoegh Line and offered monthly sailings to Karachi, Bombay, Cochin, Colombo, Madras and Calcutta. Up to twelve passengers were carried onboard large freighters such as the *Hoegh Dyke*. West German-built, this 17-knot ship was especially designed to carry vegetable oils, liquid latex, lube oils and other liquids. (Gillespie-Faber Collection)

Hopeville

Norway's A. F. Klaveness & Company sailed as the Klaveness Line – with ships such as the *Bronxville, Bonneville, Bougainville, Hopeville* (shown here in Brooklyn) and *Sunnyville* – and operated a long-haul service to the Far East and Southeast Asia. (Port Authority of New York & New Jersey)

Hrvatska

Built as the *St Lawrence Victory,* this 7,600-tonner was sold to Jugolinija in 1947, renamed *Hrvatska* and refitted with seventy-five passenger berths for Rijeka–Mediterranean–New York service. Seen here in a photo dated 30 June 1959, the 455-ft-long *Hrvatska* was teamed with another small combo ship, the *Srbija,* the former German freighter *Crostafels* which had been refitted for forty-four passengers in two classes. (Richard Faber Collection)

Indiana

'I came from Sweden to New York on the freighter *Indiana*. It was a ten-day trip from Gothenburg to Brooklyn,' remembered Anna Lundquist,

It was cheaper than a liner and allowed more luggage. I was traveling with two small children as well. The officers were very pleasant, the food good and the days undemanding and restful. Fortunately, it was summer and the seas were quite calm. On an August morning, I had my very first glimpse of the famous New York skyline. I just kept staring. I was in America, my new home, and walked ashore from Pier 97.

(James McNamara Collection).

Indochinois

Outbound from Pier 88, the *Indochinois* was actually a combination passenger-cargo ship temporarily used after the Second World War in French Line's Le Havre–New York freighter service. In this view, the Con Edison gas tank, located at the foot of West 44th Street and Twelfth Avenue, is also seen. Something of a harbourside landmark, it was erected in the 1930s, but pulled down in 1968. (James McNamara Collection)

Inger Skou

Freighters from Denmark's Skou Line, such as the *Inger Skou*, often came to New York as part of charters. Alcoa used them to carry bauxite up from South America while Cunard often employed by them to supplement their Liverpool–New York and London–New York freighter services. The smart-looking *Inger Skou* is seen here berthed at Port Newark on 28 July 1966. (James McNamara Collection)

Israel (above)

For some years, Israel's Zim Lines had to be content with a pier at the foot of Kent Street in Brooklyn's distant Greenpoint section. Created along with the state of Israel itself, Zim made do at first with secondhand ships until West German reparations programs underwrote the building of new ships. Constructed at Hamburg in 1955/6, the 9,600-ton *Israel* and her sister *Zion* were fine, 313-passenger combo liners used on the Haifa–Mediterranean–New York run. The 501-foot long *Israel* is seen outbound along the East River. (Gillespie-Faber Collection)

Jesenice (overleaf)

Photographed on her maiden arrival in 1960, the 9,500-ton *Jesenice* had a top speed of 21 knots. This allowed for rather fast, ten- to fourteen-day passages between Rijeka and New York with calls at other Mediterranean ports. (Gillespie-Faber Collection)

Kamperdyk

In addition to its luxury liner operations, Holland America Line offered a freighter service across the North Atlantic – mostly to Antwerp and Rotterdam, but sometimes beyond to Bremen and Hamburg. The 7,200-ton *Kamperdyk* was one of five sisters – *Kinderdyk*, *Kloosterdyk*, *Kerkedyk* and *Korendyk*. (James McNamara Collection)

Kinkasan Maru

'The *Kinkasan Maru* belonged to Mitsui-OSK Lines, which berthed over in Brooklyn,' remembered Captain McNamara. 'They were fast ships for their time, making up to 20 knots. Mitsui-OSK had distinctive colouring – light blue hulls with pinkish smokestacks. Ships like the *Kinkasan Maru* carried breakbulk cargo with some containers on deck.' (James McNamara Collection)

Korean Exporter

'The *Korean Exporter* is getting her picture taken, in front of the north tower of the World Trade Center, which was in the earliest stages of construction, in 1968,' noted Captain McNamara. 'Korean had bought lots of Manchester Line freighters, but the *Korean Exporter* was among the first of their newbuilds.' (James McNamara Collection)

Kristen Brovig

The Mexican Line chartered mostly Norwegian freighters for its services out of New York and other US East Coast ports. 'The *Kristen Brovig* was ideally suited to the Mexicans. She was a small Norwegian freighter with a small, but adequate cargo capacity,' noted Captain McNamara. This 1959 view shows the ship arriving in New York for the first time. (James McNamara Collection)

Lago Argentino

The successor to the Argentine State Line was the ELMA Lines, Empresas Lineas Argentinas, which built a new series of ships such as the 8,900-grt *Lago Argentino*. 'They were quite delightful ships,' according to Captain McNamara. 'They were well run, very efficient and all the officers wore uniforms. ELMA was a very fine, state-run company.' (James McNamara Collection)

Laust Maersk

Maersk ships were well-known in New York harbour, with their blue hulls and ship names painted along the sides. Two or three Maersk freighters called each week and often had special on-board facilities for Asian-made silks, reefer space and deep tanks for a variety of liquid goods. In this 1959 view, it is something of a special occasion – the 6,400-ton *Laust Maersk* has just arrived on her maiden voyage, at Brooklyn's Pier 11. Across the shed is her sister ship, the *Marit Maersk*, while an older fleetmate, the *Jeppesen Maersk*, can be seen to the left. Today, Maersk is the largest container-cargo operator in the world. (Port Authority of New York & New Jersey)

Limon

Upon arriving in New York and proceeding along the Hudson River, the handsome, usually all-white ships of the United Fruit Company were at the first piers along the lower end of the Manhattan waterfront. The company used piers at the foot of Morris and Rector Streets. In this view, the elegant *Limon* awaits a Friday afternoon sailing for Central America. (Gillespie-Faber Collection)

Loida

'The *Loida* was an enlarged Liberty ship shown here loading excavators for mining, in a view dated June 1963,' noted Captain McNamara. 'With a United Fruit ship in the background, the *Loida* is docked at Pier F, Jersey City, and has an Erie Railroad barge alongside and an M. P. Howlett goose-neck floating crane.' (James McNamara Collection).

Loide-Colombia

Commissioned in March 1947, the 443-ft-long *Loide-Colombia* was one of twenty identical sisters built for Brazil's Lloyd Brasileiro. She is seen here at her berth at 30th Street, Brooklyn, and about to take on two Bucyrus-Erie power shovels from a car float. The date is 16 June 1960. These Lloyd Brasileiro freighters traded between New York and ports in Brazil. The 17-knot *Loide-Colombia* was scrapped in 1969 in Spain. (Gillespie-Faber Collection)

Losmar

Calmar Steamship Company was in the inter-coastal trade, between the US East Coast and West Coast. 'Owned by Bethlehem Steel, which was in the steel business as well as in ship building and ship repair, Calmar operated six–eight ships, all of them named for places. As examples, the *Portmar* was named for Portland, the *Marymar* for Maryland and the *Losmar* for Los Angeles. Calmar ships in the '50s were specially modified Liberty ships, each fitted with taller masts and longer booms, which were useful for loading timber in the Columbia River. The extended booms could reach over the decks. These ships carried steel from Baltimore to the West Coast and then timber from the West Coast. They loaded general cargo when available and at New York, from the Chelsea Piers and later Port Newark.' (James McNamara Collection)

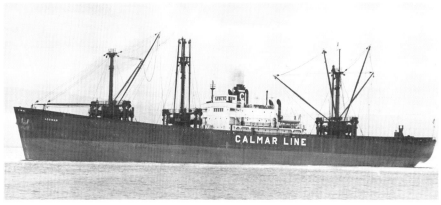

Lubumbashi

'The *Lubumbashi* and her sisters were absolutely gorgeous ships,' said Captain McNamara. 'They were beautiful ships for any trade. They were always impeccable and carried twelve passengers in great comfort. The *Lubumbashi* was used in the African trade, bringing in bales of rubber and nuts. Until the 1960s, the Belgian Line docked at Piers 14 and 15, at the foot of Fulton Street in Lower Manhattan.' (James McNamara Collection)

Ludwigshafen

After the Second World War, the Hamburg America Line and North German Lloyd jointly operated their freighter operations to and from New York. The services were looked after by a shipping agent, the US Navigation Company. North German Lloyd also resumed its passenger liner service (in 1955), but the Hamburg America Line did not. The *Ludwigshafen* is shown here in August 1954, arriving off Brooklyn. (James McNamara Collection)

Manchester Miller

Britain's Manchester Lines ran a service between New York, other US East Coast ports and Manchester. There was a disruption, however, when in December 1968 the *Manchester Miller* had a fire in one of her cargo holds while berthed at East River Pier 36.
(James McNamara Collection)

Manila

Belonging to the Maritime Corporation of the Philippines, the aptly named *Manila* makes a winter arrival.
(James McNamara Collection)

Marine Courier

'The *Marine Courier*, a Liberty ship, is being serviced at anchor in the Lower Bay by two barges and a pair of M. P. Howlett goose-neck floating cranes,' noted Captain McNamara. 'She is discharging salt to be used for winter roads and streets in and around New York City. The *Marine Courier* was specially modified as a bulk carrier for Marine Transport Lines, the successor to the old Mallory Lines.' The date of this photo is 11 March 1957.
(James McNamara Collection)

Marine Leopard

Completed in early 1946, the *Marine Leopard* joined the Luckenbach Lines in 1961 and became the *Edgar F. Luckenbach*. She was used in the inter-coastal service between the US East Coast and West Coast and is seen here in February 1958. Luckenbach later pulled out of shipping and concentrated on its shoreside, terminal operations. The 524-ft-long ship was later sold to States Marine Lines and her name changed in 1968 to *Overseas Edgar*, and then a year later to *Overseas Daphne*. She was broken up in 1972.
(James McNamara Collection)

Mellum

Flying the West German flag, the 5,000-ton *Mellum* is seen arriving on her maiden voyage. Shown passing under Manhattan Bridge, on the East River, she was bound for the Kent Street pier located in Greenpoint, Brooklyn. She would be used in New York–South American charter service.
(James McNamara Collection)

Minnesota

The Swedish Transatlantic Line added four new sisters in 1965: *Minnesota* (shown here), *Indiana*, *Alabama* and *Arizona*. 'These Swedish motor ships carried lots of wood pulp from Sweden to New York,' recalled Captain McNamara. 'These ships also served Finnish, Danish and Polish ports.' (James McNamara Collection)

Mississippi Lloyd

'These sturdy ships, such as the *Mississippi Lloyd* seen on her maiden arrival, had superb accommodations for passengers as well,' noted James McNamara. They sailed between US East and Gulf coast ports and the Middle East as well as to Indonesia for Nedlloyd, the Dutch combination of the Nederland Line and Royal Rotterdam Lloyd. Outwards, their ships carried general cargo including chemicals and heavy lifts; on the return trips, they were loaded with the likes of jute, burlap and carpet backing.' (Gillespie-Faber Collection)

Mohammed Ali El Kebir

Egypt's Khedivial Mail Lines used the long Columbia Street pier in Brooklyn in later years for its twin, converted Victory ships, the *Cleopatra* and *Mohammed Ali El Kebir* (shown here). They had been restyled after the Second World War to carry up to seventy-five passengers each. They offered monthly service to the Mediterranean – to Marseilles, Genoa, Naples, Beirut and Alexandria. This was later extended to include Karachi and Bombay. (Gillespie-Faber Collection)

Monte Albertia

Until the 1960s, Spain's Naviera Aznar offered an irregular service between Bilbao and New York. Ships such as the veteran *Monte Albertia*, built in 1931, carried general cargo on the westbound voyages and often berthed at the Ninth Street pier in Hoboken. Once unloaded, the vessel would be shifted over to Port Newark, also in New Jersey, to load scrap metal that would be brought to Spain for recycling. The scrap metals would be loaded from barges and lifted aboard by goose-neck floating cranes.
(Gillespie-Faber Collection)

Monte Ulia

Naviera Aznar owned a number of passenger-cargo liners, such as the 210-passenger *Monte Ulia*, which were used in regular service between England, Spain and the Canary Islands or farther afield, to the east coast of South America. On occasion, however, and with the passenger quarters sealed off, the likes of the 10,123-grt *Monte Ulia* would cross to load a cargo of scrap metal. (Richard Faber Collection)

Mormacdawn

Moore McCormack Lines, one of New York's largest and best-known shipping lines, also operated a subsidiary, the American Scantic Line, for north European service. This operation generally used the larger, C3-Class *Mormacdawn* and her sisters, each carrying up to twelve passengers and routed between New York, Oslo, Gothenburg and Copenhagen. (James McNamara Collection)

Mormacfir (left)

Moore-McCormack, commonly referred to as Mor-Mac, were primarily interested in South American passenger and freight services. For the freighters, the firm offered two sailings per week. The mainline service sailed to Rio de Janeiro, Santos, Montevideo and Buenos Aires; the secondary run was to Belem, Fortaleza, Recife, Bahia and Rio de Janeiro. Here, the Victory Class *Mormacfir* is being docked at Pier 32 at the foot of Canal Street in Lower Manhattan. Ward Line's *Oriente* is just behind, docked at Pier 34. (James McNamara Collection).

Mormacsea (overleaf)

In the early 1960s, Moore-McCormack consolidated its freight operations at Manhattan's Pier 32 and in Brooklyn Heights to a new terminal at 23rd Street. It could handle six freighters at one time. The C2-Class *Mormacsea* is at the outer end.
(James McNamara Collection)

Neder Weser

The combined services of Holland's Nedlloyd Lines were noted for their long voyages out to the Middle East and Southeast Asia. Often, their ships carried heavy equipment and large steel products, and so big, sturdy freighters were the order of the day. The 10,959-grt *Neder Weser*, commissioned in 1960, was one of them. Along with over 700,000 cubic feet of general cargo space, her heavy lift booms could handle loads of up to 175 tons. Neder is a brief forename for the ship's actual owners, the Amsterdam-headquartered Nederland Line. (James McNamara Collection)

Newberry Victory

For many years, Prudential Lines used Victory ships on its transatlantic freighter trade. Each Friday, ships such as the 7,600-grt, 17-knot *Newberry Victory* cast off for ports in the Mediterranean – to the likes of Casablanca, Barcelona, Genoa, Naples and Piraeus. (Norman Knebel Collection)

New York Star

Britain's Blue Star Line was part of the consortium that included the likes of Ellerman Lines, New Zealand Shipping Company and the Federal Line, which ran monthly sailings between New York (usually Port Newark) and ports in Australia and New Zealand. A new addition, the 463-ft-long *New York Star* joins the team and is seen at the time of her maiden arrival off Lower Manhattan on 1 February 1966. (James McNamara Collection)

Noordam

Every Saturday at noon, either the *Noordam* or *Westerdam* departed from Holland America Line's 5th Street pier in Hoboken on a direct, nine-day sailing to Rotterdam. A combo liner, the *Noordam* (shown here) carried 134 all-First Class passengers in high standard quarters. In her six holds, she often arrived with cheeses, tulip bulbs and cases of Dutch beer. The 10,726-grt *Noordam* is seen arriving off Hoboken in a view dated 14 September 1955.
(Gillespie-Faber Collection).

Obuasi

At a prominent position along the upper Brooklyn waterfront, the 5,900-ton *Obuasi* of Britain's Elder Dempster Lines is departing from Pier 1, at the foot of Fulton Street. The ship is departing for exotic West Africa, to ports such as Takoradi, Lagos, Freetown and Accra. She is carrying American manufactured goods and will return with the likes of bark, roots and palm oil. The scene dates from 6 October 1961.
(Port Authority of New York & New Jersey)

Oriental Queen (below)

'C. Y. Tung's Oriental Overseas Line was made up mostly of secondhand freighters in the 1960s,' recalled James McNamara. 'But the *Oriental Queen* was among the first of the Company's newbuilds. She was a beautiful-looking, ultra-modern ship for 1969.'
(James McNamara Collection)

Panama (opposite)

In this 1957 view of two of the splendid Panama Line passenger-cargo ships, the 493-ft-long *Ancon* is on the left and her twin sister, the *Panama*, on the right. These ships, carrying up to 216 all-First Class passengers, made Tuesday or Friday afternoon departures on fourteen-night itineraries to Port au Prince and Cristóbal. They were operated until 1961 by the Panama Line or, more formally, the Panama Steamship Company.
(Port Authority of New York & New Jersey)

Paola Costa

Italy's Costa Line offered a weekly freighter service between Brooklyn and ports in the western Mediterranean: Barcelona, Marseilles, Genoa, Livorno and Naples. A number of their ships were secondhand, such as the 6,500-grt *Paola Costa*, which had been the *Peter Maersk* of the Maersk Line.
(James McNamara Collection)

Parthia

Cunard's combo liners *Media* and *Parthia* (shown here, arriving on her maiden voyage in April 1948) would usually arrive on Saturday, on direct crossings from Liverpool, and then depart on the following Friday. In later years, they would often be seen berthed on the north side of Pier 92 at West 52nd Street. Each ship carried considerable cargo as well as 250 passengers. (Richard Faber Collection)

Pia Costa

Improving their services to and from the Mediterranean, Costa Line added the rather splendid, engines-aft *Pia Costa* and her twin sister *Maria Costa* in 1958. Each 551-ft-long ship carried a dozen passengers on their runs to the Mediterranean and made calls at Philadelphia, Baltimore and Norfolk. According to Captain McNamara, 'The design of the engines-aft *Pia Costa* was borrowed from the American C4-Class. These ships, the first new builds for Costa, had lots of tanks as well as heavy lift capabilities.' (James McNamara Collection)

Pioneer Mill

A division of the far larger United States Lines, American Pioneer Line offered sailings every ten days in the late 1950s on the long-haul run to the Far East. Large, fast Mariner Class freighters carrying twelve passengers were routed from New York City's Pier 61 to the Panama Canal, Honolulu, Manila, Hong Kong, Keelung, Kobe or Yokohama and Pusan. Passage fares in 1957 from New York to Hong Kong were posted at $400.

The 564-ft-long *Pioneer Mill* was one of the Mariner Class freighters that were built by the Maritime Administration just after the Korean War, in 1953/4. These ships, with no less than seven hatches, were considered to be among the finest freighters afloat at the time of their construction. Built as the *Show Me Mariner*, but actually laid up for her first two years, she joined United States Lines in 1956 for their American Pioneer operation to the Far East. She was rebuilt in 1970 as the enlarged containership *American Alliance*. The 20-knot ship was sold for scrapping in 1985, a year before a bankrupt United States Lines closed down. (James McNamara Collection)

President Grant (opposite, top)

Pier 9 in Jersey City, unused by deep-sea ships for almost two decades, became part of the Newport Center project of high-rise apartments, office towers, vast shopping malls and waterfront parks and marinas in the late 1980s. It was all part of a great renewal project of otherwise abandoned, derelict industrial properties. It was all a great blemish on the face of New York harbour. In high enthusiasm, Pier 9 was to be rebuilt as a museum, perhaps for Jacques Cousteau's undersea explorations. That project lagged, however, and then, on a windswept night in March 1994, fire burnt out the far end of old Pier 9. Demolition of the entire shed followed.

The great American President Lines was the pier's long-time tenant. Constructed in 1929, the company's two finest and largest passenger liners, the 22,000-ton sisters *President Coolidge* and *President Hoover,* called their on their extended maiden voyages out to the Far East via the Caribbean, the Panama Canal, Mexico and California. Other, smaller passenger-cargo ships, such as the seventy-eight-passenger *President Garfield,* sailed in continuous around-the-world service, outwards across the Pacific and to the Orient; home through the Mediterranean and across the Atlantic.

After being used by wartime transports and troopships, San Francisco-headquartered American President resumed its passenger and cargo services from Jersey City in 1946. Two well-appointed combo liners, the all-First Class, ninety-six-berth sisters *President Monroe* and *President Polk*, ran regular 100-day world cruises. A set of twelve-passenger freighters such as the *President Grant* (shown here) ran to the Far East and back, and another group of these cargo liners sailed on two- and three-week inter-coastal voyages to Havana, the Canal Zone, Mexico and then up to San Diego, Los Angeles and San Francisco. A trio of rather splendid, new sisters for the world cruise run were planned in the early 1950s, but these were sequestered by the federal government for trooping duties in the Korean War.

The eventual changeover to more efficient containerised shipping required far more space, different facilities and equipment and therefore a move, in the late 1960s, to the vast dockland of Port Newark, New Jersey. But just before, in March 1966, the company's largest cruise ship, the *President Roosevelt*, made a call at Pier 9 as part of a luxurious circumnavigation that sailed west-about. Afterward, the Finnlines used Pier 9 for a short time before it turned completely to storage and a mooring to out-of-work barges.

The brown brick-clad ventilator for the Holland Tunnel still stands at the outer end of Pier 9. It is, in a way, a last reminder of those long-ago, busy days of American President Lines in Jersey City. (Gillespie-Faber Collection)

President Jackson (opposite, bottom)

With quarters for twelve passengers, the Mariner Class freighters of American President Lines were said to be among the most luxurious of their kind afloat. Along with spacious cabins, a lounge and dining room, these ships had a passenger elevator and observation lounge. They were used in the ninety-five-day around-the-world service and called regularly at Pier 9 in Jersey City.

The 564-ft-long *President Jackson*, built in 1953, started life as the *Volunteer Mariner*, sailing under charter to the Matson Line. Sold to American President in 1955 and rebuilt at Baltimore as the *President Jackson,* she later (in 1972) became the *Joseph E. Hewes* for the Waterman Steamship Company. Days for this 9,600-tonner ended in 1980 in the scrapyards at Kaohsiung in Taiwan. (James McNamara Collection)

President Monroe

American President's most diverse service were ninety-five-day voyages westbound voyages around the world. In addition to superbly decorated Mariner Class cargo liners carrying up to twelve passengers each, the sisters *President Monroe* (shown here, having just departed from Pier 9 in Jersey City) and *President Polk* carried ninety-six all-First Class passengers. The final leg of these itineraries included a westbound transatlantic service from Alexandria, Naples, Genoa, Marseille and Leghorn. Leghorn to New York took eleven days.
(Moran Towing & Transportation Company)

Prinses Margriet

Holland America Line chartered and then bought the 116-passenger *Prinses Margriet* from other Dutch owners, the Oranje Line, in 1963. First used on the Rotterdam–New York run (to replace the Holland America's *Noordam*), this small combo liner was later used by Royal Netherlands for New York–Caribbean service. (Alex Duncan)

Prudential Seajet

'The *Prudential Seajet* and her sister, the *Prudential Oceanjet*, were variations of the *American Racer* class of freighters belonging to United States Lines,' noted James McNamara. 'Prudential was owned by Spyros Skouras, from the movie family, and these two ships were the first newbuilds for Prudential.' The 565-ft-long *Seajet* is seen here on her maiden arrival, in the lower Hudson River. The pair was later sold to the Grace Line. (James McNamara Collection)

Republica de Colombia

Commissioned in 1965, the big, brand-new *Republica de Colombia* and her sisters were created by the state-owned Grancolombiana, the national shipping line of Colombia, to strengthen its services to ports such as Cartagena, Santa Marta and Buenaventura. (James McNamara Collection)

Republica del Ecuador

While the great majority of Grancolombiana's ships were under the Colombian flag, this 11,600-tonner was thoughtfully placed under the Ecuadorean flag. (Gillespie-Faber Collection)

Rio Aguapey

Based at Pier 25 at Franklin Street in Lower Manhattan, the Argentine State Line ran three splendid combo liners as well as a fleet of freighters. The freighters, such as the 7,600-grt Victory Class *Rio Aguapey*, ran monthly voyages between New York and Buenos Aires. (James McNamara Collection)

Rio de la Plata (1951)

At 11,000 tons, the Italian-built *Rio de la Plata* and her two twin sisters, the *Rio Jachal* and *Rio Tunuyan*, carried up to 116 passengers in all-First Class quarters. These 550-ft-long ships tended to arrive on Saturdays and then sail on Friday afternoons for Rio de Janeiro, Santos, Montevideo and Buenos Aires (on the return, northbound voyages, they included Trinidad and La Guaira). The full round voyage took six weeks. The ships offered fine accommodations that include modern public rooms, a lido deck, outdoor pool and cabins with private and semi-private bathroom facilities. (Gillespie-Faber Collection)

Robin Sherwood

Robin Line was a division of the Moore-McCormack Lines. With their silver-painted masts and booms, dove grey hulls and often unusual funnels, their ships were quite distinctive in New York harbour. They operated from Brooklyn's Erie Basin. In the '60s, however, Robin was further integrated into Mor-Mac's operations and lost its identity.

The 7,200-grt *Robin Sherwood* was typical of the mass-produced American freighters of the Second World War. Ordered by the Robin Line in 1941, she was converted to a troop transport in 1943 and then rebuilt as a freighter after the war ended, in 1946. Like many others, she finished her days (in 1970) at the hands of scrappers on Taiwan (James McNamara Collection)

Rubens

In addition to their New York–Antwerp service, the Belgian Line – or, more formally, Compagnie Maritime Belge – ran a service dubbed the Belgian African Line. It was routed from New York to St Vincent (in the Cape Verde Islands) and then to Matadi, Luanda and Lobito in the Congo. In the late 1950s, passengers were carried on the fifteen-night voyages to Matadi for $475. In this view, the brand-new, 9,000-grt *Rubens* arrives on her maiden call at New York. (James McNamara Collection)

Sagaholm (opposite)

In the early 1960s, Swedish American Line added four new cargo liners, which included the 6,916-grt *Sagaholm*, shown here arriving on her maiden voyage in August 1963. (James McNamara Collection)

Santa Elisa

On Friday afternoons in the 1950s and '60s, the proud passenger liners of the once very popular Grace Line departed. With steam whistles sounding, the sisters *Santa Rosa* and *Santa Paula* alternated their departures for the warm waters of the Caribbean. They ran thirteen-night itineraries, calling at Curaçao, Aruba, Kingston, Port au Prince and Port Everglades. There were splendid ships which were yacht-like with intimate quarters and only a mere 300 passengers; they departed from Pier 57 in New York City. Located at the foot of West 15th Street in the city's now much-gentrified Chelsea section, these days the pier has seen happier and certainly better days. The exterior is scarred and rusting in places, graffiti artists have done some work and numerous broken windows hint of closure and abandonment. With its gleaming stainless façade facing onto the mighty Hudson, the 900-ft-long terminal might see better, renewed days in future. There are plans of the day to make the city-owned property over as a museum, shops, food markets, small theaters and other public spaces. Cost of renewal ranges from $200 million.

In its day, the pier was an engineering marvel and a highlight to an otherwise aging, worn city waterfront. The adjacent Chelsea Piers dated from 1907–10. The earlier Pier 57, used until the 1930s by the French Line, burned down in 1947 and so had to be replaced. The steamship business was booming and Manhattan boasted no less than 100 operative piers jutting out like fingers. The new Pier 57 was built on a trio of floating, concrete caissons that were actually constructed upriver, at Haverstraw, New York, and then, in the care of a fleet of tugs, floated down the Hudson. This technology was inspired by the floating caissons used for beach landings in the Second World War.

The new Grace Line terminal formally opened in February 1954 and was highlighted not only by the most advanced cargo handling methods (Grace Line had over two dozen ships, mostly freighters, in its US–Latin American services) as well as the novelty of rooftop parking for both passengers and staff. Grace occupied adjoining Pier 58 as well and, on those Fridays and wanting to avoid high weekend dockers' overtime, no less than four Grace Line ships usually departed before 5 p.m. on Friday afternoons.

Business, as well as shipping, was changing by the 1960s, especially with the inception of speedy container operations. Grace moved south to Pier 40, at West Houston Street, and shared with the likes of the Holland America, Norwegian America and German Atlantic lines, in 1969. Pier 57 was transferred over – to a non-shipping role as the city's MTA, the Metropolitan Transportation Authority – for use as a bus garage and maintenance facility. They finally moved out in 2004. The three-storey pier has been empty ever since.

In this view (overleaf), the 1944-built *Santa Elisa* departs from Pier 58. (James McNamara Collection)

Santa Magdalena

Between 1963 and '64, Grace Line added four quite unique passenger-cargo containerships – the *Santa Magdalena, Santa Maria, Santa Mariana* and *Santa Mercedes* – for their weekly service to the west coast of South America. Because of their containerized cargos, they required more open, specialised berths, and so used berths out in distant Port Newark. Ships such as the 547-ft-long *Santa Magdalena*, seen here arriving on her maiden voyage in February 1963, carried 125 passengers in luxurious quarters.
(Moran Towing & Transportation Company)

Santa Olivia (overleaf)

Ships such as the 8,500-ton *Santa Olivia* often departed from New York with as much as 3,500 tons of American manufactured goods, including lots of heavy machinery. On her inbound trips from South America, the 459-ft-long, 1946-built ship would arrive heavily loaded with Chilean melons, Colombian coffee, copper ingots and as many as 75,000 stems of bananas.

As a temporary berth, Grace used Pier 45 at West 10th Street in New York City's Greenwich Village when its Pier 57 burned in 1947. Here, we see the *Santa Olivia* arriving with the *Santa Isabel* on the other side of the shed. (James McNamara Collection)

Santa Rita

West Germany's Hamburg-South American Line traded as the Columbus Line for its US East Coast–South America service. Ships such as the handsome-looking *Santa Rita* were assigned to a run from Brooklyn's Erie Basin to Recife, Salvador, Rio de Janeiro, Santos, Montevideo and Buenos Aires. The *Santa Rita* dated from 1954. (James McNamara Collection)

Santa Rosa

During disruptive, often long, maritime strikes, ships would gather in New York harbour. Sailings would be cancelled and ships idle. Here, in this 1964 view, we see the Bethlehem Steel shipyard in Hoboken. Four noted passenger liners are laid up: *Independence* (left), *Constitution*, *Santa Rosa* and *Santa Paula*. In the top right are at least two of Grace Line's fifty-two-passenger combo ships.

Built in 1958, the *Santa Rosa* and *Santa Paula* carried 300 all-First Class passengers each. (Hoboken Historical Museum)

Santa Sofia

'The *Santa Sofia* and her eight sisters were among the finest combo ships of their time,' noted Captain McNamara.

They carried up to fifty-two passengers each, had air-conditioned dining rooms and outdoor movie screens attached to their aft masts. Three were used in Caribbean service and the other six on the Grace run to the west coast of South America as far south as Valparaiso. Usually, two of this class sailed every Friday along with one liner (either the *Santa Rosa* or Santa *Paula*) and one twelve-passenger freighter. The *Santa Sofia* and her sisters maintained fairly regular schedules and carried general cargo as well as the likes of heavy mining equipment on their southbound runs and returned with the likes of copper, bananas and coffee. Sometimes, they would offload copper in Perth Amboy, New Jersey, which is some 30 miles southwest of New York harbor.

(James McNamara Collection)

Sarah Bowater

The little green-hulled freighters of the Bowater Company carried large amounts of newsprint down from Newfoundland to New York. Ships such as the *Sarah Bowater* used Pier 96, located at the foot of West 56th Street and convenient for the nearby printing plant of the *New York Times*. (Gillespie-Faber Collection)

Savannah

The US government was anxious to promote the peaceful use of atomic energy in the 1950s, and among the projects was the building of the nuclear-powered combo liner *Savannah*, commissioned in 1962. This 15,000-ton ship was advanced in design and carried cargo as well as sixty all-First Class passengers. First used by States Marine Lines, the 595-ft-long vessel was soon shifted to American Export-Isbrandtsen Lines and used mostly on the New York–Mediterranean run. Unfortunately, she was unsuccessful in many ways and was decommissioned in 1971. She became a museum for a time, was then mothballed, and most recently (2015) she is moored in Baltimore harbour, awaiting conversion for further museum operations. Normally docked bow-out for security and safety reasons, this view shows the *Savannah* at Pier B, Hoboken, in 1965. (James McNamara Collection)

Seatrain New Jersey

Edgewater, New Jersey, located some 5 miles north of Manhattan and along the western shores of the Hudson, was home to freighters carrying Ford automobiles, tankers and, most prominently, the railway car-carrying ships of the Seatrain Lines. Formed in 1929 and based in Hoboken until 1940, ships such as the uniquely configured *Seatrain New Jersey* could carry the equivalent of 1 mile of freight cars on voyages to ports such as Savannah, New Orleans, Galveston, Texas City and Havana. A huge, oversized crane loaded and offloaded these rail cars between ship and pier. In the face of containerisation, Seatrain pulled out of this trade in the early 1970s and dabbled in container freighters and even into shipbuilding at the former Brooklyn Navy Yard until it collapsed altogether in 1981. (James McNamara Collection)

Selfoss

From their terminal at Pier F in Jersey City, the Icelandic Steamship Company offered twice-monthly sailings to Reykjavik. Twelve passengers were carried along with general cargo on the outbound sailings and large loads of frozen fish on the inbound voyages. Assisted by a McAllister tug, the 3,500-grt *Selfoss* is arriving at Pier F at Harborside Terminal. (James McNamara Collection)

Silvaplana

'This ship was Swiss-owned and uniquely registered in Basel. They were called "the ships that could never go home",' recalled James McNamara. 'They were bulk cargo ships, but which ran an irregular service to New York.' The 13½-knot *Silvaplana* dated from 1956.
(James McNamara Collection)

Sir John Franklin

From 1 July 1949 until 30 June 1950, 7,950 vessels entered New York harbour, arriving from forty-two different countries. Clearing the harbour in the same period were 8,114 ships. Among them was the *Sir John Franklin* of the Isbrandtsen Line, shown leaving Brooklyn Heights for a four-month trip around the world.
(James McNamara Collection)

Steel Advocate

Until the 1960s, the Isthmian Lines offered five distinct freighter services from their large terminal at Brooklyn's Erie Basin. There was an India–Pakistan–Ceylon service; Mediterranean–Red Sea run; Persian Gulf service; around the world service with emphasis on Southeast Asia, and, in a joint operation with the Matson Line, a run to Hawaii via the Panama Canal. Here we see the C3-Class *Steel Advocate*.
(James McNamara Collection)

Steel Traveler

'Isthmian was a division, until 1955, of United States Steel and then afterward owned by States Marine Lines,' added Captain McNamara. 'There were twenty-four C3-Class freighters used in service between the US East Coast, the Middle East, the Persian Gulf, Indonesia and Hawaii. Isthmian pulled out of the freighter trade in 1973, however. One of the last of their C3 freighters, the *Steel Traveler* finished her days at the hands of Taiwanese scrappers in that same year.' (James McNamara Collection)

South African Transporter

The South African Marine Corporation, the Safmarine Lines, offered a joint service with the States Marine Lines on ships that included accommodations for up to twelve passengers. The 1951-built *South African Transporter* ran voyages from New York (Brooklyn) to Cape Town, Port Elizabeth, East London, Durban and Lourenço Marques. Passage fares on the three-week voyages to Cape Town began at $330 in the late '50s.
(Gillespie-Faber Collection)

Strathaird

While one of the world's great shipowners, P&O was not an especially well-known name in and around New York harbour. They did appear, with freighters such as the *Strathaird*, for services to the Middle East and India. (James McNamara Collection)

Suffren

French Line strengthened their Le Havre–New York service with two new sisters in 1967: the 9,900-ton *Suffren* (seen here) and the *Rochambeau*. The 19-knot *Suffren* is seen arriving on her maiden voyage on an otherwise foggy morning off Lower Manhattan. She later berthed in Brooklyn. (Gillespie-Faber Collection)

Suruga Maru

Trade between New York and Japanese ports resumed in 1951 and grew steadily. By the 1960s, it began to boom. To support its services between Yokohama, Kobe and New York, the NYK Line added a new series of 9,500-ton freighters. Here we see the *Suruga Maru* and with a twin sister, the *Sagami Maru*, just behind berthed at Pier 7 in Brooklyn. The date is January 1962. The *Francesco 'C'* of Costa Line is just beyond and then a freighter on the South American run for the Norton Line. (James McNamara Collection)

Tahsinia

Britain's Anchor Line ran passenger liners between Glasgow and New York until 1939, but then resumed in 1946 with freighters only. Their sailings were often coordinated with Cunard cargo ships. The *Tahsinia* is seen here at Swedish American Line's Pier 97 in this 1959 photo. (Gillespie-Faber Collection)

Tervaete

The Victory Class *Tervaete* was used in a regular, nine-day service between New York and Antwerp for the Compagnie Maritime Belge, better known in Manhattan shipping circles as the Belgian Line. These ships berthed at Piers 14 and 15 at Fulton Street in Lower Manhattan. The New York Telephone, Woolworth and Transportation buildings are in the background.
(Port Authority of New York & New Jersey)

Tetela

Operated by an affiliate of United Fruit, the handsome-looking 'banana boat' *Tetela* was owned by Empresa Hondurena de Vapores and flew the Honduran flag. 'These Dutch-built ships were beautiful and always very, very clean,' noted Captain McNamara. 'Southward, they carried general cargo plus plantation supplies and cardboard for banana boxes and then sailed northward with full loads of bananas.'
(James McNamara Collection)

Transmariner

'The *Transmariner* was a C-1 Class steamer [some others were diesel-driven] that belonged to American Union Transport Lines. They were used in their service between New York and Puerto Rico,' recalled Captain McNamara. 'It is rather ironic that she is carrying Sea-Land containers in this late 1950s view before Sea-Land began its own service to Puerto Rico. Based on Staten Island, AUT later became Transamerica Trailer Transport, TTT for short, and went from breakbulk to trailer ships.'
(Gillespie-Faber Collection)

Tannstein

By the mid-1950s, North German Lloyd was rebuilding with brand new freighters, replacing the massive Second World War losses and with post-war Allied construction restrictions lifted. The 5,500-grt *Tannstein* had her debut in 1955 and improved the company's Bremerhaven–north Europe–New York service. (James McNamara Collection)

Tian Hai

Chinese freighters were rare visitors in the 1960s and '70s, but there were occasional calls. Here we see the *Tian Hai* loading scrap metal for Far East ports while at Port Newark. (James McNamara Collection)

Toluca

'TMM, the Mexican Line, did not need large freighters for New York–Mexico service and so smaller, secondhand ships such as the 4,000-grt *Toluca* suited their needs,' said Captain McNamara. 'She was the perfect three-island freighter with a wooden deckhouse and crew quarters aft.' (James McNamara Collection)

William Patterson

Newsworthy! Repowered with a history-making free piston gas turbine and sporting a new bow, the converted Liberty ship *William Patterson* became an example of reviving wartime-built Liberty ships in case of a national emergency. Now capable of 17 knots, about 7 knots more than her original speed, the *Patterson* – to be operated by the Lykes Lines – came to New York for 'show off' purposes. Dressed in flags and carrying officials and members of the steamship community, she set off on a short demonstration cruise on 18 September 1957 from United States Lines' Pier 61. (James McNamara Collection)

Uhenfels

West Germany's Hansa Line were best known for their heavy-lift ships, handling large industrial cargos. Ships such as the 10,400-grt *Uhenfels* had a useful engines-aft design, practical for large deck cargos, as well as heavy-lift cranes. Hansa traded to the Middle East – via Suez from New York to Djeddah, Port Soudan, Djibouti, Aden, ports in the Persian Gulf, Karachi, Bombay, Colombo, Madras, Calcutta and Rangoon. 'Hansa Line freighters often carried railways cars, especially old steam engines that were retired in the 1950s and '60s by American railroads and that were sold for further service in the Middle East. These freighters also carried oil company cargos including big cooling towers. They also carried a few of the early containers, some of which were placed forward in the bow section.' (James McNamara Collection)

Vretaholm

In addition to their liner service with the likes of the *Stockholm, Kungsholm* and *Gripsholm,* the Swedish American Line ran a weekly service with twelve-passenger freighters between New York and Gothenburg. In 1958, the ten-day crossing was priced from $235 in high summer and from $195 in winter. The freighter *Vretaholm* is seen here berthed at Pier 97, at West 57th Street in New York City. (Richard Faber Collection)

Whakatane

In 1960, to supplement services to Australia and New Zealand, the mighty, 8,400-grt *Whakatane*, belonging to the British-flag New Zealand Shipping Company, arrived from Auckland and Wellington via the Panama Canal. She delivered a large cargo of frozen meats and wool to the Norton Lilly terminal at Port Newark. (James McNamara Collection)

Wolverine State

A large C4-Class freighter, the 12,000-grt, 520-ft-long *Wolverine State* was commissioned just after the Second World War ended, in September 1945, but as the *Marine Runner*. A decade later, she became the *Wolverine State* and began serving for States Marine Lines on their New York–Le Havre–Southampton run. She is here in a photo dated 1964 and with the mighty Verrazano-Narrows Bridge nearly complete. The ship was not broken up until early 1972, at Kaohsiung on Taiwan. (James McNamara Collection)

Wonosobo

The Nedlloyd Line was a combination of two large Dutch shipowners: the Nederland Line and Royal Rotterdam Lloyd. It offered twice-monthly departures from Brooklyn's Bush Terminal on ships such as the 7,500-grt, twelve-passenger *Wonosobo* on long voyages to the Suez Canal and then onward to Bahrain, Kuwait, Abadan, Khorramshahr, Basrah and finally an optional call turnaround at Calcutta. Passage fares on the three-week voyage to the Persian Gulf were listed as $550 in the late 1950s. The Dutch owners also ran the Java–New York Line service to Indonesian ports and Singapore, as well as an African service. The *Wonosobo* is seen here in a view off Brooklyn dated 4 September 1955. (James McNamara Collection)

Yozgat (below)

Immediately after the Second World War, in 1946/7 many American-built Liberty and Victory Class freighters, among others, were declared surplus. Quite new vessels, they were either sold or given to much-depleted nations for renewal and rejuvenation. Here, at the Second Street pier in Hoboken, we see two Victory ships – the *Gorun* (left) and *Yozgat* being refitted for service with the Turkish Maritime Lines. They will be used in New York–Istanbul service as well as between ports within the Mediterranean. (Richard Faber Collection)

Zion (overleaf)

Zim Lines had to make do for many years with a terminal over at the foot of Kent Street along Brooklyn's inconvenient Greenpoint waterfront. Finally, in 1962, they were able to move to Manhattan, to the former Panama Line Pier 64, at the foot of West 24th Street. Two years later, they moved south to Pier 32, Canal Street, which had been vacated by the Moore-McCormack Lines. In this aerial view, we see the 9,600-ton combo liner *Zion* arriving for the first time at Pier 64 in April 1962. (Richard K. Morse Collection)

BIBLIOGRAPHY

Hornsby, David, *Ocean Ships* (Shepperton, Surrey: Ian Allan Ltd, 1982).

Jaffee, Walter, *The Freighters From A to Z* (El Cerrito, California: The Glencannon Press, 2010).

Le Fleming, H. M., *Ocean Ships* (London: Ian Allan Ltd, 1962).

Miller, William H., *Going Dutch: The Holland America Line Story* (London: Carmania Press Ltd, 1998).

Miller, William H., *Great American Passenger Ships* (Stroud, Gloucestershire: The History Press Ltd, 2012).

Miller, William H., *Great Ships in New York Harbor* (Mineola, New York: Dover Publications Inc., 2005).

Miller, William H., *Merchant Ships of a Bygone Era* (London: Carmania Press Ltd, 1997).

Miller, William H., *New York Shipping* (London: Carmania Press Ltd, 1994).

Miller, William H., *Pictorial Encyclopedia of Ocean Liners, 1860-1994* (Mineola, New York: Dover Publications Inc., 1995).

Miller, William H., *The Last Blue Water Liners* (London: Conway Maritime Press Ltd, 1986).

Moody, Bert, *Ocean Ships* (London: Ian Allan Ltd, 1971).

NYK Maritime Museum. Yokohama, Japan: NYK Line, 2005.

Official Steamship Guide.

Towline.